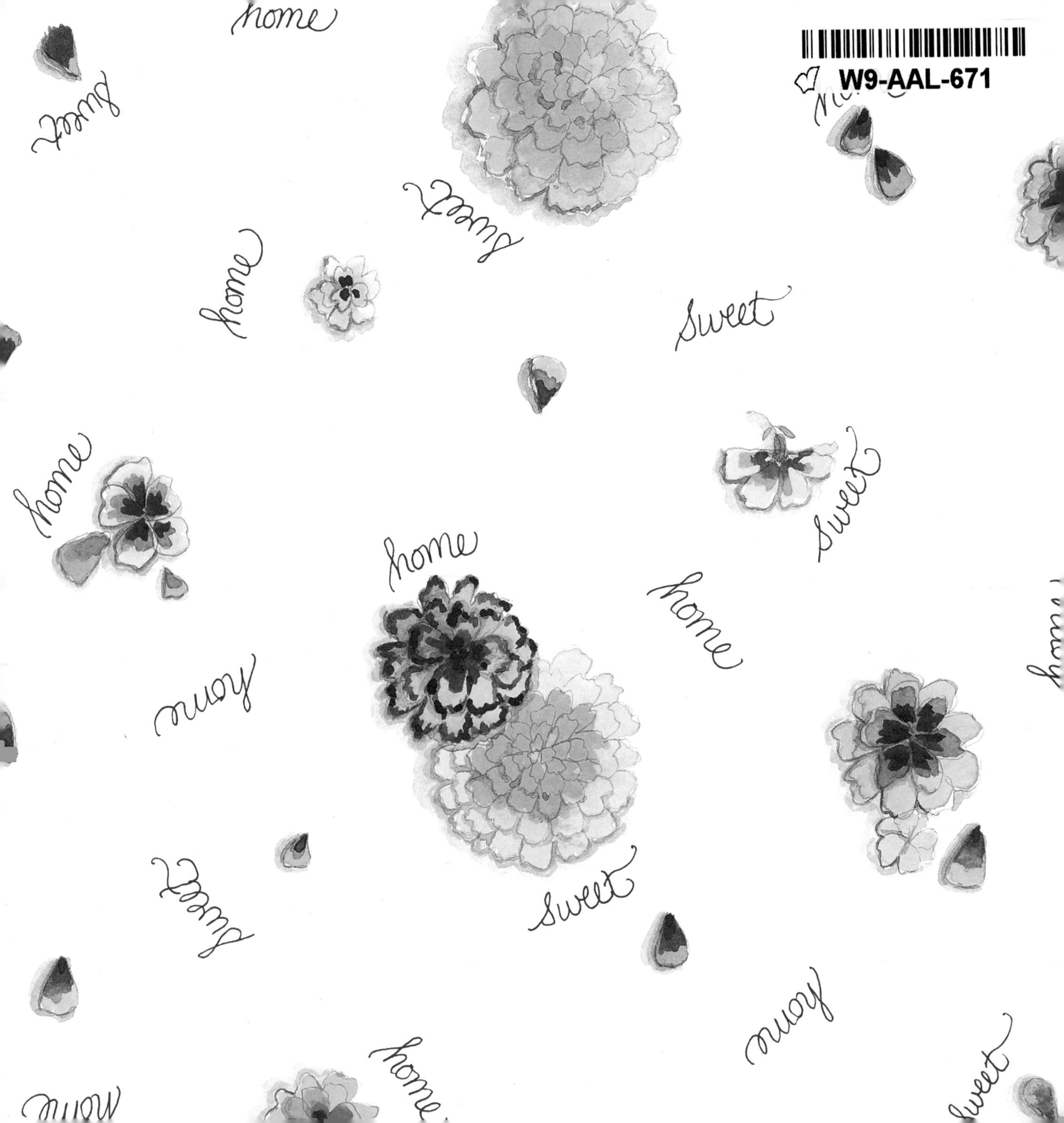
home
sweet
home
sweet

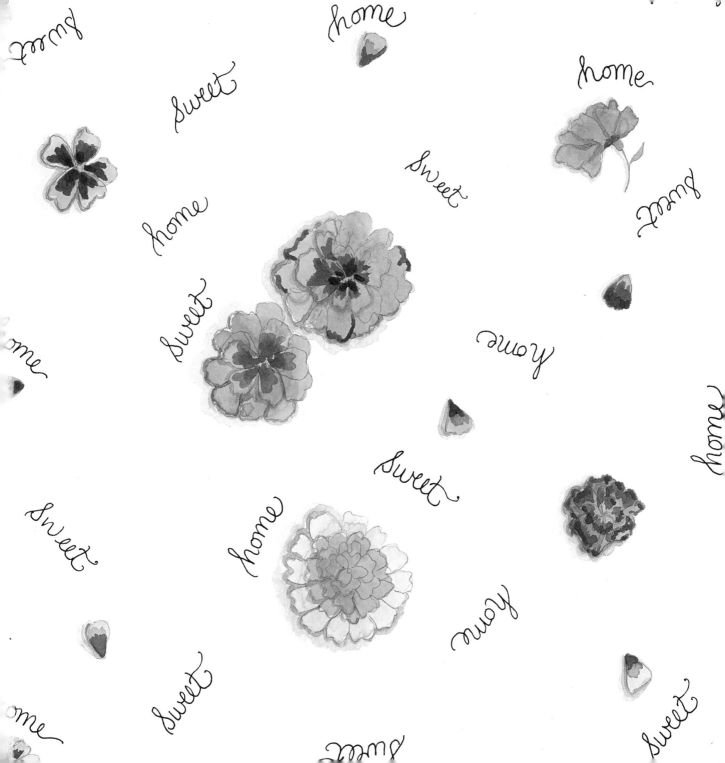

The Blue Bowl ~

REWARD

All day I did the little things,
The little things that do not show;
I brought the kindling for the fire
I set the candles in a row,
I filled a bowl with marigolds,
The shallow bowl you love the best~
And made the house a pleasant place
Where weariness might take its rest.

The hours sped on, my eager feet
Could not keep pace with my desire.
So much to do, so little time!
I could not let my body tire;
Yet, when the coming of the night
Blotted the garden from my sight,
And on the narrow, graveled walks
Between the guarding flower stalks
I heard your step: I was not through
With services I meant for you.

You came into the quiet room
That glowed enchanted with the bloom
Of yellow flame. I saw your face,
Illumined by the firelit space,
Slowly grow still and comforted~
"It's good to be at home," you said.

BLANCHE BANE KUDER ♥

Welcome Home

Simple Tips For Turning Your House Into a Luxurious Retreat

This Book Belongs To : _____

"Home's not merely four square walls
Tho with pictures hung & guilded;
Home is where affection calls,
Filled with shrines the
Heart
hath builded."
CHARLES SWAIN

Welcome Home

Simple Tips For Turning Your House into a Luxurious Retreat

"The dearest spot on earth to me is home, Sweet home."
W.T. WRIGHTON

Copyright © 2004 by Melissa Placzek

♥ First Edition ♥

♥ First published in the USA in 2004
by
Fair Winds Press
33 Commercial Street
Gloucester, MA 01930 ♥

Library of Congress Cataloging-in-Publication
Data Available

ISBN 1-59233-056-8 ♥
10 9 8 7 6 5 4 3 2 1
Book & Cover design by
Melissa Placzek
PRINTED AND BOUND IN CHINA

Dedicated to my Family
Jeff, Andrea, Grace & Miller Cat

The People that make my house a home...

Thank you for believing in me

Famous Red Wing Flower Baskets ♥

On a sunny day in June of 1999, Jeff & I took a little road trip to charming Red Wing Minnesota, to do some house shopping. Our dream was coming true! We were about to become HOME OWNERS!

I'll never forget the first time we saw our Victorian cottage. We knew we were home the minute we walked through the front door. When we stepped out the back door and saw the rose garden we just knew the house was blessed. ♥

I want to dedicate this book to my wonderful little family. My husband Jeff & my daughters Andrea & Grace... and Miller Cat. I love you all!

Table of Contents

There's no place like HOME...

♥ At the end of each chapter are journal pages

Hydrotherapy
Spa Hand Therapy with Warming Mitts
Rosemary Foot Bath
Strawberries & Champagne Foot Spa
Marble Foot Massage
Romantic Edible Massage Oil
Romantic Edible Honey Dust
Beach Babe Suntan Oil
Maui Lip Gloss
The Spirit of Scent
"Put the Lime in the Coconut" Perfume Mist
Baby Bubbles : Little Luxuries for Your Little Love
Home Sweet Home Room Mist
Lemon Mint Window Wash

Spa Breakfast Apple Coffee Cake
Festive Fruit Gazpacho
Thai Chicken Pita Pizza
Leaning Tower of Pisa Spinach Lasagna
Easy Spa Dessert Ideas

"Shut the door. Not that it lets in the cold, but that it lets out the coziness." MARK TWAIN

Creating Ambience While You Cook

Cooking the evening meal is one of my favorite things to do. I light candles in the kitchen, play a soothing CD, and sip on a glass of wine as I cook. I like to have a colorful bouquet of flowers or a bowl of tangy lemons on the counter to delight my senses when I pass by. In warmer months, I open our back porch door so I can listen to the birds singing and the wind chimes tinkling and smell the fresh air as I create my culinary masterpieces. I like to wear comfortable, flowing cotton clothes when I cook, and I always go barefoot. Naked feet are a must. ☺ I also love to write the evening's menu on a big "bistro" board that I made out of a large blackboard, and display in our dining room.

Using exotic ingredients is one of my favorite simple pleasures. Cheese from Provence, wine from Italy, spices from India, chocolate from Switzerland, & unfiltered extra virgin olive oil from Spain. I also like to use fresh ingredients every day. Herbs & vegetables from my kitchen garden, baguette from our village bakery, sausages & meats from the local butcher, and freshly squeezed fruit & vegetable juices.

"There is no sight on earth more appealing than the sight of a woman making dinner for someone she loves." THOMAS WOLFE ♥

THE KITCHEN
THEMES & DECORATING IDEAS ♥

"Strange to
see how a
good dinner
and feasting
reconciles
everybody."
SAMUEL PEPYS ♥

The Art of Keeping a Kitchen Journal ♥

In the late eighteenth & early nineteenth century, women kept kitchen journals as diaries, cookbooks, and a place to record kitchen notes & homekeeping tips. Because keeping a home is an art as well as a science, I believe the kitchen journal could also be a useful tool in today's modern homes. And they are so fun to make! Here are some of a kitchen journal's uses:

♥ A daily diary to record experiences & dreams ♥ A place to record favorite family recipes, home remedies & cleaning tips ♥ A nature sketchbook & flower press ♥ A place to diagram your garden(s) & keep a list of your favorite plant varieties and ones you would like to try. ♥ A place to keep a wish list of things you would like for your home, and a list of decorating ideas ♥ A list of favorite cookbooks ♥ Entertaining notes (to record guest lists, menus and party theme ideas) ♥

A kitchen journal would make a beautiful family heirloom to pass down to future generations. What a treasure! Some day your children and grandchildren can use your journal to re-create your time-honored ideas in their homes.

Kitchen journals and cookbooks were the first books published by women in the USA. Here are a few of my favorites: *Miriam's Cookbook* by Carrie Bender; *Kentucky Housewife* by Lettice Bryan; and *Savoring the Past* by Barbara Ketcham Wheaton.

"Food provides you with an unbroken thread which links you to your ancestors."
— ANONYMOUS

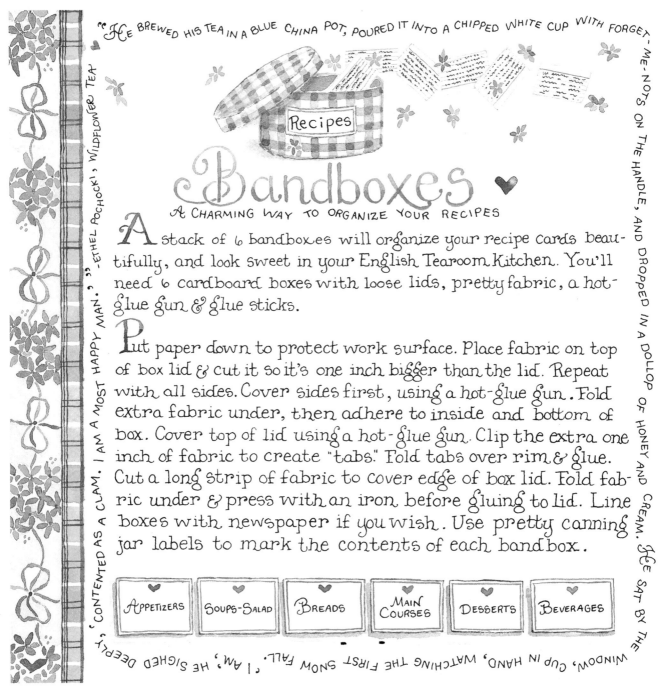

Recipes

Bandboxes ♥

A CHARMING WAY TO ORGANIZE YOUR RECIPES

A stack of 6 bandboxes will organize your recipe cards beautifully, and look sweet in your English Tearoom Kitchen. You'll need 6 cardboard boxes with loose lids, pretty fabric, a hot-glue gun & glue sticks.

Put paper down to protect work surface. Place fabric on top of box lid & cut it so it's one inch bigger than the lid. Repeat with all sides. Cover sides first, using a hot-glue gun. Fold extra fabric under, then adhere to inside and bottom of box. Cover top of lid using a hot-glue gun. Clip the extra one inch of fabric to create "tabs." Fold tabs over rim & glue. Cut a long strip of fabric to cover edge of box lid. Fold fabric under & press with an iron before gluing to lid. Line boxes with newspaper if you wish. Use pretty canning jar labels to mark the contents of each bandbox.

| Appetizers | Soups-Salad | Breads | Main Courses | Desserts | Beverages |

Wine Bottle Stoppers & Stem I.D. Rings

Wine bottle stoppers & stem I.D. rings make great little party favors or hostess gifts. While you have probably noticed that you can spend a small fortune on them in specialty gift shops, the ones you make yourself will only cost a few dollars at the craft store, and are much more original and personal when made by your own hands.

WINE BOTTLE STOPPERS: Apply a strong industrial strength glue (such as super glue) to the top of a new bottle cork. Press a flat sided, decorative knob on top of the cork. Apply pressure to the knob for a few minutes. Let glue set for 48 hours.

STEM I.D. RINGS: Purchase thin wire ring hoops, small beads, and charms from your local craft store or jewelry making store. Add the beads & charms to the hoops. Voila! It's really THAT easy! ☺

"Wine is bottled poetry."
ROBERT LOUIS STEVENSON

Herbes de Provence Baguette Spread

1 cup cream cheese
6 Kalamata olives, chopped fine
2 Tablespoons dried prosciutto
1/4 teaspoon dried rosemary
1/4 teaspoon rubbed sage
1/2 teaspoon dried basil
1/8 teaspoon dried lavender

Mix all together in a small bowl.
Chill until ready to serve.
ENJOY! ☺

Sonoma County
Red
Cabernet Sa...

Shopping at Ethnic Markets

"FROM GREENLAND'S ICY MOUNTAINS, FROM INDIA'S CORAL STRAND, WHERE AFRIC'S SUNNY FOUNTAINS ROLL DOWN THEIR GOLDEN SAND." ~ REGINALD HERBER Missionary Hymn

ITALY & FRANCE

ITALY: espresso, wine, pastas of all shapes, spicy deli meats, sauces, truffle oil, truffle honey, and the BEST leather shoes and purses.

FRANCE: perfume, baguette, pastries, chocolate, every kind of cheese known to man, heavenly bed linens, olive wood, olive oil, Provence linens, soaps, art & lavender

ASIA

green tea & teapot sets, hand fans, chopsticks, silk, sake and sake sets, paper shoes, paper lanterns, porcelain rice bowls, yummy noodles and soups, rice paper journals and stationery, cardboard take-out boxes, bamboo placemats, steamers, large paper parasols

This is your passport to exotic lands! Ethnic shopping is the next best thing to taking a vacation. The aromas, sounds, vibrant colors, textures, & flavors are a feast for the senses and will change the way you look at shopping forever. Here are some of my favorite countries to explore, and lists of the goods they specialize in. *Bon Voyage!*

MEXICO

blankets, hand blown glassware, piñatas, ponchos, sombreros, hot sauces, salsas, mole sauce, strings of dried hot chilies & garlic, terra cotta, pottery, fresh tortillas, chimineas (outdoor, patio fireplace), silver, turquoise, pure vanilla, cocoa, pan dulce, and the ingredients for homemade tamales!

INDIA

curry, exotic spices, basmati rice, saffron, saree material and other luxurious fabrics, floor cushions, wall hangings, handcrafted jewelry boxes, jewelry, exotic bedding, marquees (colorful party tents), cotton goods, wonderful massage lotions & body care goods, gorgeous rugs, incense

Teacup Candle

Fill the teacups you want to turn into candles with hot water. Melt pieces of paraffin wax in a double boiler over a medium flame just until melted. Remove wax from heat once it is melted. Pour the hot water out of the teacups and dry them thoroughly. Carefully pour melted wax into cups and allow them to set until a soft covering appears on top of wax. Push a birthday candle into the wax so it stands straight. Add a little glitter to the tops of candles. Allow candles to harden completely before burning.

Tea tips: tea bags relieve puffy eyes, remove the odor of fish or onion from your hands by rubbing them with wet tea leaves.

"I don't drink coffee. I take tea, my dear."
~STING

16

Window tea-herb garden

FOR A TON OF INFO. ON HERBS READ THE "RODALE HERB BOOK" (BY 7 HERB GURUS ☺)

A little tea-herb garden is so simple to create & care for. Being able to reach for fresh, fragrant herbs at teatime is such a pleasure, you will wonder where this tiny garden has been all your life ☺

Plant a tea-herb garden by first selecting containers such as baby-sized teacups & terra cotta pots. Make a mixture of 3 parts rich soil & compost, 1 part sand, a little bone meal or ground oyster shells, & some wood ashes.

Once herbs are planted, set containers on a tray of pebbles. Pour a bit of water over pebbles (so they are half covered in water.) This will provide a cool, moist atmosphere for your garden. Place tray in a south facing window. Water herbs when soil feels slightly dry. Mist leaves twice a week.

♥ Tea Sandwich Herbs ♥
Watercress
Basil
Nasturtiums
Dill
Parsley
Chives
Rosemary

cucumber - dill mmmm...!

nasturtiums

♥ Tea Infusion (Tisane) Herbs ♥
Mint
Chamomile
Lavender
Lemon Verbena
Goldenrod
Sassafras
& Borage as a garnish ☺

Shaped Strainer :: Thanks Phillip!

Earth Friendly Farmer's Market Tote

good deed for the day ♥

Cut a piece of prewashed and dried, sturdy fabric into a 36 × 18 inch rectangle. Some good fabrics for this project would be vintage bark cloth, ticking, or canvas. Give the two short edges a narrow, rolled hem so they don't fray. Fold the fabric in half, right sides together, so the two finished edges meet. Sew along right and left sides with a ½ inch seam allowance. Cut two pieces of Shaker tape to the length you would like your handles to be. Pin the handles in place. Sew each end onto the tote as shown in Figure "A". Turn the bag right side out and use for your farmer's market or grocery store outings.

Fig. "A"

"The lovely thumping pumpkins and squash, the rosy onions and reliable potatoes are stored. Apples fill the barrels. Cabbages come in. The freezer is filled to the top with all the summer produce, and the jellies, jams, pickles, and relishes are stored in the fruit cellar." ~ Gladys Taber ♥

In Your Own Words
J O U R N A L

"Garlic is the ketchup of intellectuals."
- ANONYMOUS

In Your Own Words

JOURNAL

ESPRESSO MACHINE

"THE COOK WAS A GOOD COOK, AS COOKS GO; AND AS COOKS GO SHE WENT." -Saki

A Sweet Retreat

lovely ideas for decorating your

BATHROOM

"Art washes from the soul the dust of everyday life."

~Pablo Picasso~

IVORY SOAP

The Seaside Bathroom Theme

"THE VOICE OF THE SEA SPEAKS TO THE SOUL." ~ KATE CHOPIN

For me, a day at the beach is a time for reflection, restoration and meditation. After reading for a couple hours and enjoying the sensual experience of clear colors, clean scents, rippling sounds & cool, crisp textures, I emerge feeling completely refreshed.

This is the same way I like to feel when I retreat to my bathroom for a soak in the tub or to enjoy an at-home spa ritual.

The seaside theme will be perfectly at home in your bathroom because the beach and the bathroom share the same focal element... water! So, why not bring the tranquil seaside theme to your bathroom? ∴ Every day could be a day at the beach!

"Ever drifting... On the shifting currents of the restless main; Till in sheltered coves, and reaches of sandy beaches, all have found repose again." -Longfellow

THE SEASIDE THEME

AT A GLANCE

Seashells * lighthouses * message in a bottle * vintage metal buckets * revolving nursery lamp with underwater images * frosted beach glass * a big scallop shell as a soap dish * clamming basket to hold hand towels * beach towels in place of bath towels * draped fishnets * glass fishing floats * indoor shutters * antique compass collection * signal flags as curtains * sand castle statues * jar hurricane lanterns * floating candle seaside scene * sail boats

"Teach me to hear the mermaids singing."
JOHN DONNE

23

Jar Hurricane Lanterns

EMBELLISH YOUR LANTERN BY SPRINKLING TINY SHELLS IN THE SAND AROUND VOTIVE CUP.

A jar hurricane lantern is created by first making a handle for the jar out of twenty-gauge iron wire. The only rule for making a good handle is being sure it holds the jar securely! ☺ Pour a little beach sand in the bottom of the canning jar. Push a glass votive cup into the sand. Set a votive candle in the cup. (Try "Seaside Holiday" scent by the Yankee Candle Company ☺ Mmmmm...) NOTE: Using a votive cup is necessary if you want to insure that no melted wax will mingle with the sand (which can be very hard to clean up! ☺)

"...NOW MY BROTHERS CALL FROM THE BAY,
NOW THE GREAT WINDS SHOREWARD BLOW,
NOW THE SALT TIDES SEAWARD FLOW;
NOW THE WILD WHITE HORSES PLAY,
CHAMP AND CHAFE AND TOSS IN THE SPRAY."

...MATTHEW ARNOLD...

Scented Seashell Potpourri

Scrub a bunch of small shells with soap & water. Dry well. Brush shells generously with the scented oil of your choice. Perfume and beautify your bathroom by displaying the seashell potpourri in a big clamshell.

"There is magic in the distance where the sea-line meets the sky."
— Alfred Noyes

Setting The Scene
Celestial Fantasy Bathroom

"... SAILING THE CELESTIAL SPACES..." J. MUIR

Picture a secluded bathchamber with twinkly candlelight, glistening gossamer, winking stars, cherubs, and rainbows dancing on the walls. These are the elements that make up the "Celestial Fantasy" theme.

Have fun creating your own cloud 9 with the oodles of ideas on the next few pages & by using a dollop of romance, a pinch of magic and a smidgen of imagination. Then... when you retreat to this sanctuary... Run a bubble bath, pour yourself a goblet of Fairy Nectar (a glass of champagne OR sparkling white grape juice + 2 drops blue food coloring :) Experience the epitome of "Calgon, take me away!" :

Celestial Fantasy Bathroom
at a glance

❤ Add floating candles & rose- ✦ petals to a full tub for a party ❤

Stars ✦ flower garlands
Clouds painted on ceiling ✿ add glitter to paint
before painting walls ✿ Candlelight ✿ gossamer
canopy over a free-standing tub ✿ celestial shell
candles (p# 45 of "Chin Deep In Bubbles") ✿ Crystals hung in
Window ♥ = dancing rainbows on your walls! ✿
fairy bouquets arranged in salt shakers or perfume
bottles ✿ magic wand ✿ strings of faux
pearls

"...The earth, and every common sight,
to me did seem appareled in celestial
light, the glory & the
freshness of a dream."
WORDSWORTH

PINK Glitter

27

Aromatherapy Window Panel
WITH ORGANZA POCKETS

Materials:
- many yds. burlap
- 1 yd. organza
- sewing machine
- scissors
- dried, fragrant flowers & herbs (such as clover, jasmine, lavender, lemon verbena, rose & geranium

petals, spearmint, & pressed pansies.)
- curtain rod
- café clips
- In autumn: replace flowers with fall leaves, cinnamon sticks, little pinecones, vanilla & coffee beans.

♥ Measure inside of window frame. Cut burlap to this size, adding 4 in. to length. ♥ Gently pull one thread from burlap piece along bottom edge. This will create fringes. ♥ To create a grid pattern on panel, cut single threads along any selvage edge to remove them from finished edges. Pull a few threads to make a skinny strip about 3/4 inch wide. Remove threads in this manner both vertically & horizontally to achieve a grid pattern. ♥ For pockets: cut squares of organza to fit into squares on the panel. Add ½ inch to edges of organza squares so edges can be folded back & stitched to the panel. ♥ Sew organza squares to panel leaving tops open to create pockets. Place flowers & herbs inside pockets. Attach panel to curtain rod using café clips.

♥ *"All wreathed with fairy fruits and flowers..."* ~ Poe

28

"Canopy of Heaven" Candle Chandelier
THE "BELLE" OF THE BATHROOM

Hello Stargazer! Now you can have your very own source of flickering "Starlight" at your fingertips!

Fashion a celestial candle chandelier to adorn your bathroom. Start with a pretty wood frame as a base. Using apoxy, adhere 4 lightweight candle cups (one at the midpoint on each side of frame.) Hot glue silk flowers & greens to frame (I love wisteria :) Add some pretty silk bows beneath each candle cup. Hang chandelier with lengths of strong ribbon securely fastened to each corner with a staple gun. Create a "loop" out of the remaining ends of ribbon. Staple to secure the loop. Place loop on one end of an "S" hook. Hang from ceiling screw with an "O" at one end.

... Blue quietness above ..."

29

The Fragrant Laundry

EASY, SCENTED LAUNDRY SOAP: Add 1 teaspoon lavender essential oil & 1 teaspoon lemon verbena essential oil to a 64 oz. bottle of unscented laundry detergent. Shake well before each use.

LAVENDER LINEN SPRAY: Wonderful for sheets, jammies, linens and throw rugs. (I even use it on my yoga mat.) In a 4-oz. glass spray bottle combine 20 drops lavender essential oil, 3 tablespoons 100 proof vodka, and top off with distilled water. Shake well. Allow to rest 2 weeks. Spray desired linens.

DRYER SACHETS: Place ¼ cup lavender flowers in a small muslin bag and tie top securely. Add to your dryer along with wet laundry. The sachet will last about 12 loads. Open sachet & refresh with 2 drops essential oil as needed.

"Exactness in little things is a wonderful source of cheerfulness."
Fredrick William Faber

In Your Own Words

J O U R N A L

"Fill your paper with the breathings of your *heart.*" -William Wordsworth

In Your Own Words
J O U R N A L

"" Where should one use perfume?' a young woman asked. 'Wherever one wants to be kissed,' I said. ""
~ Coco CHANEL

Blissful Bedrooms

"Titania, come sit thee down upon this flowery bed."

~ Shakespeare, "A Midsummer Night's Dream"

Do you love floral patterns & fresh, clear colors? Interior designer & author, Alexandra Stoddard, says, in her wonderful book _Feeling at Home_, "I would live in a garden if I could ... All of us who are passionate about flowers can think of our rooms as gardens." I heartily share this philosophy! After all,

Secret Garden Bedroom

Why let an overcast day get us down if we have gorgeous garden prints & hues of grass green and sky blue to brighten our walls & furniture and lift our spirits? As you peruse the next few pages imagine a pretty garden

♥ setting the scene ♥

path. Welcome to your very own Secret Garden ...

"So transform the bleak and the barren into welcoming places where one can live seems to me an important and worthwhile goal in life."

MARK HAMPTON

Secret Garden Bedroom
at a glance

♥ seed packs decoupaged to a lamp base ♥ Sheri's birdcage reading lamps (see "little luxuries" section) ♥ picket fence headboard ♥ an antique hankie & painted clothespin valance ♥ real bird nests ♥ bird houses ♥ a "moveable feast" picnic basket... include: wine & corkscrew, crackers, a tiny sealed wheel of sharp cheddar cheese, little sealed jars of jam, chocolates, a little spreading knife, 2 wine glasses & napkins ♥ lilac or gardenia essential oil to scent room ♥ a brand new bird bath as a magazine "basket" ♥ lantern votive holders ♥

"Beauty is an accumulation of details, the kind of layering that takes a long time."
— HÉLÈNE DAVID

♥ a painted clothespin & antique hankie valance

35

Graceful Gossamer Canopy

"Enjoy the honey-heavy dew of slumber." SHAKESPEARE

This is a decorating MIRACLE I tell ya! Hang a grapevine wreath on the wall, centered above your bed, about 3 feet above your headboard. Next drape gossamer bridal netting through the grapevine wreath so it hangs evenly over the sides of your bed and "puddles" on the floor. (Buy about 7 yards of the soft, shimmery netting that is used to make bridal veils.♥) I did this in my daughter Andrea's room and it took about 5 minutes. I just had to pass this one on to you! ♥

"All one really needs is a divinely attractive bed."

MRS. WINSTON GUEST

"The divine took his seat at the breakfast table, and began to compose his spirits by the gentle sedative of a large cup of tea, the demulcent of a well buttered muffin, and the tonic of a small lobster."

Thomas Love Peacock ♥

A Cozy Breakfast Nook
lattice screen

Jeff constructed our lattice screen by laying 2 pre-painted & framed lattice pieces side by side. Then he connected them with 3 hinges. He set the lattice screen up behind a little breakfast table in the corner of our bedroom. This is one of my hands-down favorite projects because it's inexpensive, quick, easy, and the end result is breath taking! ♥ A little bit of silk wisteria hung along the top of the screen and a little lamp on the table will complete the look. You'll feel like you're staying in a romantic B&B in the country. ♥

One of our favorite "Cozy Breakfast Nook" treats:

ORANGE HONEY BUTTER - Combine ½ cup REAL butter, ⅓ cup clover honey & 2 Tablespoons orange juice concentrate. Beat until smooth. Serve on pancakes, scones or muffins. YUM! ::

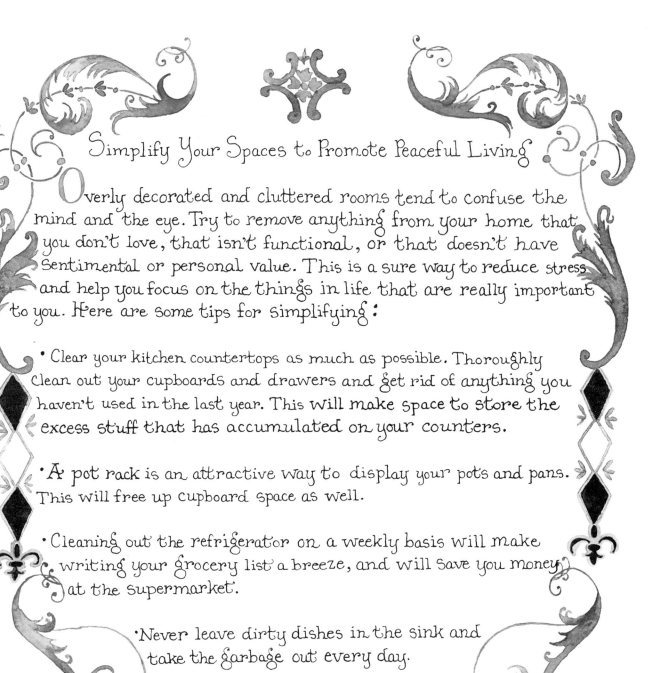

Simplify Your Spaces to Promote Peaceful Living

Overly decorated and cluttered rooms tend to confuse the mind and the eye. Try to remove anything from your home that you don't love, that isn't functional, or that doesn't have sentimental or personal value. This is a sure way to reduce stress and help you focus on the things in life that are really important to you. Here are some tips for simplifying:

• Clear your kitchen countertops as much as possible. Thoroughly clean out your cupboards and drawers and get rid of anything you haven't used in the last year. This will make space to store the excess stuff that has accumulated on your counters.

• A pot rack is an attractive way to display your pots and pans. This will free up cupboard space as well.

• Cleaning out the refrigerator on a weekly basis will make writing your grocery list a breeze, and will save you money at the supermarket.

• Never leave dirty dishes in the sink and take the garbage out every day.

• Use a set of stacking boxes or lidded baskets for keeping change, keys, receipts, lists, and other doodads out of sight.

• Start a file box for magazine articles. This is a fun thing to do while watching T.V. in the evening, and a file box full of favorite articles is much less bulky than keeping whole magazines.

• A stack of vintage suitcases makes a handsome endtable and gives you another space to hide stuff. This is where I keep paperback books.

• Armoires instead of open shelving systems. Hide the clutter. ☺

• Shallow, open-topped, wood boxes on casters make perfect under-the-bed storage units. Use them to store clothes that are out of season.

• Make your bed every morning. It is much more relaxing to get into a bed that is made.

• Do a load of laundry every day instead of letting it turn into an overwhelming pile.

• Use a flat-topped, wooden trunk as a coffee table. More storage space! YAY! ☺

"Elegance is more often achieved by what you leave out." - ALEXANDRA STODDARD ♥

♥ Romantic faux four-poster bed

Does your bed need a makeover? Add a touch of romance to your bedroom by fashioning this easy and inexpensive faux four-poster bed. Breezy, lightweight fabric, or even flat sheets hung through circular finials will help you create your romantic getaway in practically no time at all. You'll need four finials with hardware for attaching them to the ceiling. Screw one above each of the four corners of your bed. Drape lengths of fabric through the finials to make a rectangle above the bed and four "posters" that will fall to the floor on the four corners of the bed. Experiment until you come up with a look that pleases you. Have fun!

"Whatever the uses of a room, it should be a world unto itself." ~ Edith Wharton ♥

In Your Own Words
J O U R N A L

"I believe in plenty of optimism
& white paint." - ELSIE de WOLFE

In Your Own Words
J O U R N A L

" I hope with all my heart there will be painting in heaven." ♥ JEAN BAPTISTE COROT

"... minute tactual intimacies; whose resumption was the essence of coming home." — JAN STRUTHER Mrs. Miniver

living room

ZEN LIVING ROOM : SETTING THE SCENE

The Zen minimalist theme encourages spiritual calm and simple rituals of quiet harmony. Some of the elements of Zen décor include :

~ Visual balance
~ Filtered light (possibly through a shoji screen, which is a lattice screen with Japanese paper glued to it.)
~ Minimal accessories
~ A clean, fresh, tranquil, serene feel. Open & airy.
~ Neutral, monochromatic color palette
~ Natural elements
~ Eastern influence (for inspiration visit a Japanese tea house.)
~ Plants

For more information on this theme, sit back with a cup of sencha and read *A Japanese Touch for Your Home*, by Koji Yagi.

"To know when you have enough is to be rich." - Lao Tzu

ZEN LIVING ROOM – AT A GLANCE

PLACE FLOWERS & FLOATING CANDLES

IN A BOWL OF WATER

GREEN TEA SERVED ON
A BAMBOO MAT

COLORFUL PAPER
LANTERNS

JAPANESE FISH BOWL WITH A
DANCING GOLDFISH INSIDE

BONSAI TREES

Tranquil Indoor Fountain

"a green isle in the sea of love, a fountain and a shrine"... - Poe

THIS IS JUST THE BASE PLAN FOR AN EASY INDOOR FOUNTAIN. MORE TUBING CAN BE ADDED TO THE PUMP SPIGOT & MORE ROCKS CAN BE STRATEGICALLY PLACED AROUND THE TUBING FOR A MORE DRAMATIC EFFECT.

1.) YOU WILL NEED A WIDE POTTERY BOWL WITH A GLAZED INTERIOR THAT HAS A FLAT BOTTOM AND THAT IS DEEP ENOUGH TO KEEP A SUBMERSIBLE PUMP UNDER WATER. A SMALL, SUBMERSIBLE PUMP CAN BE PURCHASED AT HOME IMPROVEMENT STORES.

2.) PLACE THE BOWL ON A LARGE PIECE OF SLATE TO PROTECT YOUR TABLETOP.

3.) DECIDE WHICH SIDE OF THE FOUNTAIN YOU WANT TO BE MOST VISIBLE AND WHICH SIDE WILL BE FACING THE WALL. PLACE THE PUMP IN THE CENTER OF THE BOWL WITH THE CORD GOING TO THE BACK.

4.) PLACE A CERAMIC OR POTTERY PLANTER WITH A DRAINAGE HOLE IN THE BOTTOM UPSIDE DOWN OVER THE PUMP SO THE PUMP'S SPOUT STICKS UP THROUGH THE HOLE. THIS CAMOUFLAGES THE PUMP & LOOKS PRETTY.

5.) DECORATE WITH STONES, STATUES & BAMBOO.

6.) ADD PURIFIED WATER TO BOWL UNTIL PUMP IS IMMERSED. PLUG IT IN & ALLOW PUMP TO GET STARTED. REPLENISH WATER REGULARLY.

HEALING WATER MUSIC...

SENTED IN IT'S

NATURE REPRE-

SEE ALL OF

...IN MY OWN HANDS I HOLD A BOWL OF TEA; I SEE

Japanese Newspaper Luminaria

CANDLELIGHT IS AN EASY & INEXPENSIVE WAY TO ADD ROMANCE & ATMOSPHERE TO A ROOM.

You're going to adore these little luminarias. Use a few in the center of your dining room table as an exotic centerpiece the next time you serve sushi.

You will need:
- Japanese newspaper
- Clear glass cylinder vase
- White glue
- Copper foiling tape
- A pressed Japanese maple leaf or a fern leaf
- Matte-finish decoupage glue
- Votive candle & candle cup

Cut a piece of newspaper to fit around vase. Wrap paper snugly around vase and glue along seam where paper overlaps. Embellish top and bottom edges of luminaria with copper foiling tape. Brush luminaria with a coat of decoupage glue. Apply leaf. Allow to dry. Apply final coat of decoupage glue. Place candle in candle cup, & place inside luminaria.

47

Tabletop Rock Garden ♥

Tabletop rock gardens are interesting coffee table decorations, as well as conversation pieces. Another great place for one of these mini gardens is your desk at the office because they are wonderful for reducing stress. Just rake patterns in the sand between meetings or while you're on the phone and see if you don't agree.

You will need:
- Unpainted, wooden tea tray with short walls all the way around it
- Primer & paint
- Fine, white sand
- Rocks, little statues, shells & a small rake

Prime the tea tray. Allow to dry, and paint desired color. (Some nice colors for this project: cream, white, sage green, or black.) Fill the tray with sand and add the rocks, statues, and shells as desired. Rake patterns around the objects for a fun, meditative activity.

"What does this garden suggest? It is a sea of sand, with a few islands thrusting up above the water."
~ Jatsuo Ishimoto

Nature Walk Living Room

BRING THE BEAUTY OF A NATURE WALK HOME...

♥ Brush leaves and pieces of grass with **clear** acrylic spray. Allow to dry. Glue leaves to home made paper, sheet music, or an old love letter. Frame. A set of 4 looks gorgeous.

♥ Arrange wildflowers & cattails in a vase. Glue tiny, pressed flowers to pillar candles.

♥ Nature Walk Collage: Use a shadow box to display dried pinecones, acorns, birds nests, feathers, Robin's egg shells, dried roses, seashells, driftwood, beach pebbles, agates, and other natural items. Embellish with nature sketches if you like.

♥ Nature Under Glass Coffee Table: Place a white table runner on your coffee table. Scatter green or autumn leaves & pretty seed packs all over table. Cover with a piece of glass that is slightly smaller than coffee table. Display pretty books on nature, gardening, and a copy of *Walden* by Henry David Thoreau on your coffee table.

♥ Hand letter or stencil a favorite quote about nature on a wall.

♥ Real potted plants or trees.

"Found the most beautiful green stone. Come immediately. Zorba."
~ TELEGRAM SENT TO NIKOS KAZANTZAKIS ONE THOUSAND MILES AWAY.

 "They will build a cottage which will be complete in all it's parts."
— HENRY HUDSON HOLLY

HOUSE  WARMING

Creating a Cozy Haven for Your Family ♥

♥ Light the first fire in your fireplace at your housewarming party. ♥ Create a weekly menu written on beautiful stationery and display in an ornate frame. ♥ Use feather beds, feather pillows & goosedown comforters. ♥ Purchase an electric tea kettle so you can have a hot cup of tea whenever you want it. ♥ Build a romantic movie library. ♥ Have *The New York Times* delivered to your door. ♥ Use Amish made furniture and quilts. ♥ Build a teacup collection. ♥ Candles, candle-chandeliers & fireplaces. ♥ Use chenille slipcovers and handmade rag rugs. ♥ Have throw blankets on hand for spontaneous cuddling. ♥ Build a "Fantasy Pantry," a "Wine Cellar," & a "Hope Chest," all described in my first book, *Chin Deep in Bubbles*. ♥ Put an antique bell on your door to announce someone's return home. ♥ Use a pie safe as a pantry if you don't have one. ♥ Fill bookcases with old books. ♥ Hang artwork that lifts your spirits. ♥ Install a ceiling fan above your bed. ♥

In Your Own Words
JOURNAL

"That's the month we planted the garden. We had delectable elevenish parties with iced tea & cookies under the crab apple tree."
♥ — TASHA TUDOR

In Your Own Words
J O U R N A L

"If I had enough ribbon, I could conquer the world." -Napoleon

SATIN TAFFETA
PON 140
No. 2
★
MADE IN U.S.A.

"GOD SEND US A LITTLE HOME, TO COME BACK TO, WHEN WE ROAM... RED FIRELIGHT & DEEP CHAIRS, SMALL WHITE BEDS UPSTAIRS ~ GREAT TALK IN LITTLE NOOKS, DIM COLORS, ROWS OF BOOKS, ONE PICTURE ON EACH WALL, NOT MANY THINGS AT ALL. GOD SEND US A LITTLE GROUND, TALL TREES STAND 'ROUND, HOMELY FLOWERS IN BROWN SOD, OVERHEAD, THY STARS, O GOD. GOD BLESS THEE, WHEN WINDS BLOW, OUR HOME, AND ALL WE KNOW." FLORENCE BONE

a prayer for a little home...

More Inspiring Ideas for

Creating a Home Retreat

Fresh Air Rooms

PORCHES, SUNROOMS, PATIOS, DECKS, GAZEBOS....

♥ Display a collection of whimsical bird houses. ♥
Set up three-panel screens for privacy. ♥ Use ticking and nostalgic camp-style fabrics. ♥ Furnish with classic, antique wicker. ♥ Decorate with rusty pieces such as lanterns, a dinner bell, or cast iron stars. ♥ Stack patchwork quilts on a distressed wooden chair for a charming look. ♥ Hang a little chalkboard and a piece of chalk next to your door so friends can leave you messages if they stop by while you are out. ♥ A candle chandelier hung above your porch table makes you feel as if you're dining with the fairies & the nymphs in a Midsummer Night's Dream. ♥ Put a pretty baker's rack on your porch and use it to store garden tools. You can also use it when entertaining guests on your porch. Use it to hold a tray of silverware, a champagne bucket, a menu board, napkins, matches, extra candles, board games, and a set of romantic, mismatched china. ♥ New, colorful rag rugs every summer. ♥ String clear, Italian al-fresco globe lights everywhere & transform your outdoor room into an Italian piazza. ♥ When in doubt, PAINT IT WHITE! :: It gives your outdoor room a fresh, summery beach house feel. ♥
Indulge in patio and deck luxuries: Adirondack Chairs, an island-made rope hammock, outdoor fountain, outdoor fireplace or chiminea, comfortable outdoor furniture, a teakwood table with a market umbrella, tiki torches, and an outdoor bar. ♥

"And they were canopied by blue sky... So cloudless, clear and purely beautiful."
— Lord Byron

54

A Room of Your Own : A Snuggery

Virginia Woolf said "Every woman needs a room of her own." I believe her. There is nothing like escaping to your own space where you can be by yourself, unwind and reflect. Here's a list of ideas for a "snuggery":

❋ Paint the walls a color that soothes you. ❋ Relaxing textures: chenille, crisp linen, flannel, silk & long loop Berber carpet. ❋ A big, comfortable chair or chaise with lots of pillows and a goosedown throw. ❋ A teapot, Harney & Sons teas, and an electric tea kettle — or an espresso pot for you coffee lovers! ❋ Fill bookshelves with books that inspire you. ❋ Blank notebooks, leatherbound journals & a correspondence box full of gorgeous stationery. ❋ Beautiful art and photographs of loved ones. ❋ A box of watercolors & a watercolor journal. ❋ Fresh flowers always! ❋ A selection of beautiful music & films (check out www.cinematherapy.com) ❋ Yankee tarts in virtually every scent imaginable & a tart burner. Some of my favorite scents are : "Carrot Cake," "Ginger & Green Tea," "Hazelnut Coffee," and "Buttercream." ❋ Good lighting and a dimmer switch. ❋ A "Foot Spa", which is a little Jacuzzi for your feet. ❋ A mini 'fridge full of your favorite treats. ❋

" In solitude we give passionate attention to our lives, to our memories, to the details around us."
— Virginia Woolf ♥

Baby Nursery
I D E A S

♥ Make a puppet theatre out of a wooden, screen door.
♥ Attatch a built-in ledge to the entire length of a wall for displaying stuffed animals and toys. Underneath the ledge, hang shaker peg racks for displaying darling little baby outfits. ♥ A child-sized bookshelf for sweet bedtime story books. Some great books for the nursery library: *Toot and Puddle*, *Goodnight Moon*, *The Carrot Seed*, *The House at Pooh Corner*, and *Guess How Much I Love You*. ♥ My favorite lullabye CD: *Sleep Baby Sleep* by Nicolette Larson. ♥ Trim a plain lampshade with miniature rickrack and cute buttons. ♥ For a quick and beautiful baby quilt, sew flannel backing to a small vintage tablecloth. ♥ Baby Time Capsule: Line a shoebox with acid-free paper, cover top and bottom with pretty wrapping paper. Inside, place a newspaper from the day baby was born, hat and wrist bands from hospital, first bib and shoes, lock of hair & first tooth baby loses. ♥ Keep squares of fabric from baby's outfits and blankets. Make a quilt from squares and give it to your child as an heirloom gift for graduation, wedding, or when they have children of their own. ♥ Baby "bubbly": Buy a bottle of champagne from the year your baby was born and present it to him/her on his/her wedding day for the wedding toast. ♥

"My baby has a mottled fist, my baby has a neck in creases; my baby kisses and is kissed, for he's the very thing for kisses." —Christina Rossetti

Bed & Breakfast-Style

GUESTROOM

A list of things to pamper your overnight guests: ♥ A sewing kit. ♥ Fresh, 300+ thread count, cotton sheets ♥ Fresh quilts ♥ Mooshy towels & washcloths ♥ Polished furniture and clean windows ♥ Guest Basket: travel-sized Crabtree & Evelyn shower gels and lotions, special shampoos, postcards from your town tied together with a piece of raffia, love stamps, stationery & envelopes, a pretty pen, a key to your house with a ribbon tied through the hole, a tin of cookies, tiny wheels of sealed cheese, fancy crackers, a couple paperback books & magazines, an itty-bitty book light, spa slippers, disposable camera, and pamphlets featuring local attractions and events. ♥ A luggage rack to stack suitcases on ♥ A fresh, seasonal flower bouquet ♥ A water carafe and a glass on their bedside stand ♥ The daily newspaper ♥ Terrycloth robe ♥ A TV stand or an armoire in the guest room with a supply of movies ♥ A boom box or stereo with a supply of CDs ♥ A small coffee-maker set up in a corner with an assortment of gourmet coffees, exotic teas, cocoas, creamers, stir sticks, and sugar packets ♥ Jar candles & matches ♥ A sachet for their drawer ♥ A fresh basket of muffins outside their door in the morning ♥ Chocolate chip cookies & milk before bed ♥

"I like to have people staying with me for a few days, or even for a few weeks, should they be content with simple joys." ELIZABETH VON ARNIM

57

Laundry Room Leisure

• A pretty, fabric-covered bulletin board for tacking laundry and stain removal tips to • A row of lined, wicker baskets for keeping clothespins, sewing items, and assorted laundry tools separated • Antique or vintage soap ads framed and hung on the wall as laundry room art • A vintage bark cloth laundry bag for every family member to keep in his/her closet • This is a room where you can be daring with color. Paint the walls kayak yellow or acid green if it pleases you. • Replace your tired ironing board cover with one made from ticking, calico, or gingham. • Use lavender linen spray while ironing and listen to a book on tape. Every time you go to do laundry you can listen to the next chapter, and you will look forward to the next laundry day! • For REALLY fresh smelling laundry, use an outdoor clothesline whenever possible. • Tips: Remember, hairspray removes ink, white wine removes red wine, shampoo removes mild grease stains and dishwasher soap removes almost anything ::

"I wonder what could be lovelier than a line of pink & jonquil rompers, gay little socks, pastel baby blankets, snowy sheets and bright bath towels blowing on the line [they] have as much beauty as a painting."

GLADYS TABER

58

Luxurious Linen Hutch

Upstairs, in the bedroom with striped wallpaper, lives a secret passion of mine. It is a tall cabinet made of oak, with glass paneled doors on the front. I call it my "Luxurious Linen Hutch." Inside I keep hundreds of vintage & antique heirloom linens, all in perfectly folded bundles, and each bundle is tied with a silk or lace ribbon. This may sound ridiculous to you, and that's okay. ∵ This is probably a project that will imme- diately seem either wonderfully romantic or too time consuming and boring to pursue. I just happen to LOVE taking all the linens out a couple times a year and listening to Bobby Darrin or Edith Piaf on the CD player while I launder the linens. I wash them all in lavender & lemon verbena, press them with a hot iron until all the wrinkles disappear in a swirl of frag- rant steam, and then fold them by category: tablecloths, tea towels, nap- kins, sheets, pillowcases, and guest towels. Then I tuck a sprig of fresh rosemary under each bow to make the hutch smell sweet. Having beautiful, time honored linens is one of my favorite things. I hope it will be one of yours too. ♥

59

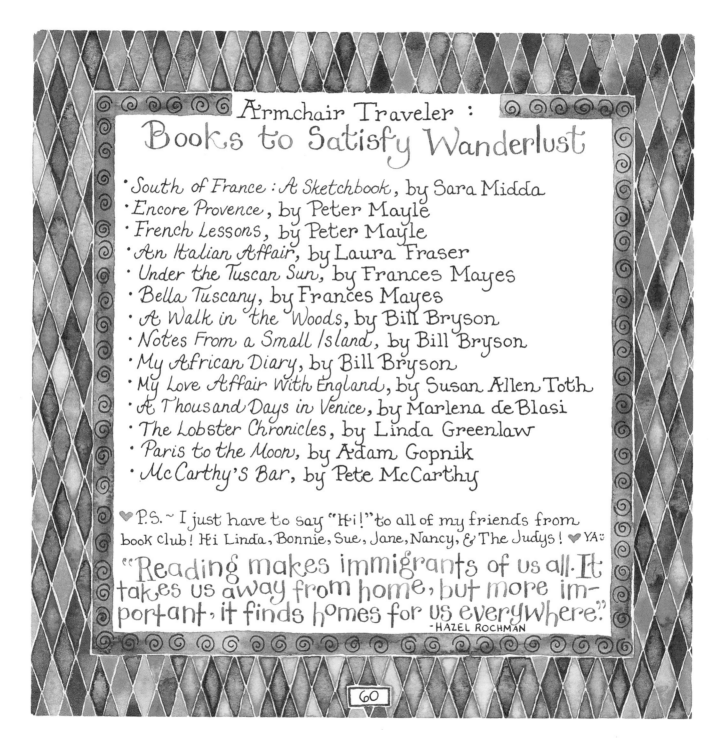

Armchair Traveler : Books to Satisfy Wanderlust

- *South of France : A Sketchbook*, by Sara Midda
- *Encore Provence*, by Peter Mayle
- *French Lessons*, by Peter Mayle
- *An Italian Affair*, by Laura Fraser
- *Under the Tuscan Sun*, by Frances Mayes
- *Bella Tuscany*, by Frances Mayes
- *A Walk in the Woods*, by Bill Bryson
- *Notes From a Small Island*, by Bill Bryson
- *My African Diary*, by Bill Bryson
- *My Love Affair With England*, by Susan Allen Toth
- *A Thousand Days in Venice*, by Marlena de Blasi
- *The Lobster Chronicles*, by Linda Greenlaw
- *Paris to the Moon*, by Adam Gopnik
- *McCarthy's Bar*, by Pete McCarthy

♥ P.S. ~ I just have to say "Hi!" to all of my friends from book club! Hi Linda, Bonnie, Sue, Jane, Nancy, & The Judys! ♥ YA:

"Reading makes immigrants of us all. It takes us away from home, but more important, it finds homes for us everywhere."
-HAZEL ROCHMAN

Home Video & DVD Library

If you've had a hard day at work and need a quick getaway, here is a list of movies for the adventurer in you- and the places these stories will take you.

Wine Country- *A Walk in the Clouds*, starring Keanu Reeves
Las Vegas- *Fools Rush In*, starring Matthew Perry & Selma Hayek
Mexico- *Like Water for Chocolate*, starring Marco Leonardi
France- *Amelie*, starring Audrey Tautou
Venice- *Bread & Tulips*, starring Licia Maglietta
Tuscany- *Under the Tuscan Sun*, starring Diane Lane
Rome- *Rome Adventure*, starring Suzanne Pleshette
Down a Rabbit Hole- *The Matrix*, starring Keanu Reeves
New York- *Annie Hall*, starring Woody Allen & Diane Keaton
Paris- *An American in Paris*, starring Gene Kelly
London- *Notting Hill*, starring Hugh Grant & Julia Roberts
Coney Island- *The Little Fugitive*, directed by Morris Engel
Africa- *Out of Africa*, starring Meryl Streep & Robert Redford
Iowa- *The Bridges of Madison County*, starring Meryl Streep & Clint Eastwood
Chicago- *Ferris Bueller's Day Off*, starring Matthew Broderick
Siam- *Anna and the King*, starring Jodie Foster & Chow Yun Fat
India- *Monsoon Wedding*, starring Naseeruddin Shah
Ireland- *Circle of Friends*, starring Minnie Driver

"You are everything I never knew I always wanted." - Matthew Perry
Fools Rush In

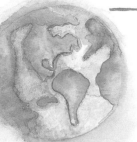

Simple Feng Shui Tips

- Play calming music and nature sounds to encourage a more soothing home environment.
- Fresh flowers will lift your spirits.
- Add mirrors to make a small room seem larger.
- Add the five elements to any room: water, fire, wood, metal, and earth.
- All televisions and stereo equipment should be housed in a cabinet with doors.
- Keep drains closed and toilet lids down when not in use.
- Choose furniture with rounded corners and place on the diagonal instead of flat against a wall.
- Only display artwork with positive images in your home.
- Make the view from your bed as peaceful as possible.
- Don't allow any clutter under your bed.
- Add candles to provide warmth, light & enchantment to a space.
- Use plants, windchimes, fishbowls with goldfish, miniature rock gardens & indoor fountains to delight and calm the senses.
- Clear all countertops and tables.

"I discovered the secret of the sea in the meditation upon the dewdrop."
–Kahlil Gibran

Soul Color Wheel

Your favorite colors say a lot about your personality and tastes. Colors can alter your mood, make a room dramatic or dull, or help you put an outfit together.

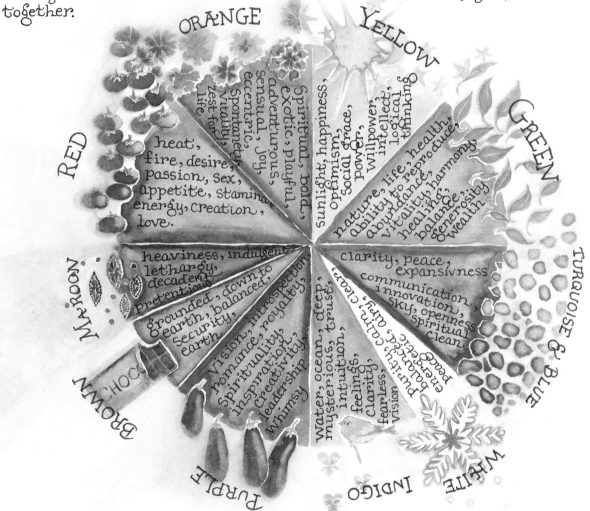

"A certain blue enters my soul, a certain red affects my blood pressure, another color wakes me up. I don't cut the oranges & reds like the greens & the blues." HENRI MATISSE

TAKE A VACATION AT HOME

"AH, THERE IS NOTHING LIKE STAYING AT HOME FOR REAL COMFORT." Jane Austen ♥

If you are anything like me, you love going on vacation. Seeing new sights, hearing new sounds, eating interesting new foods, and absorbing the feel and textures of a new place. Sometimes, however, the act of getting there can be daunting and expensive. Packing suitcases, setting up a babysitter for the kids, the hassle of airports, delayed flights, and then the endless laundry when you get home – who needs it? Here is a refreshing thought. How about taking a vacation at home this year? A home vacation can satisfy your desire for the much needed retreat that you deserve without the stress and jet lag. If this sounds appealing to you, here are some tips you can follow to enjoy your home vacation to the fullest.

♥ Hire a maid service to come in and clean your house from top to bottom the day before your vacation begins, and unplug your phone and email.

♥ Eat out at a different restaurant every night. Explore new cultures through cuisine. How about an Afghani restaurant? Sit on floor pillows and watch belly dancers while you feast on curried lamb and yogurt cake by candlelight. Other fun restaurants might include an authentic Italian where they serve everything family style, or an outdoor French café where you can sip wine and munch a baguette while you people watch.

64

♥ Pick up some brochures at your local visitors bureau and visit your own city as a tourist. Plan a fun activity every day. Go see a movie or a play. Attend a concert in a park or an art festival. Go to a gallery. Take a long bike ride and stop for a picnic. Go to a local spa for professional massages. Have a candlelight dinner. Go to the opera, a musical, or even your local Barnes & Noble to talk and sip mochas while looking at your favorite magazines. Take time to reconnect with your love.

♥ Do NOT do any home projects or anything work related. Pretend your home is a B&B. Sleep in, put your feet up, read a book.

♥ Look through family albums and scrapbooks together. Reminisce.

♥ Make sure you set aside plenty of time for relaxing. Take lots of hammock naps and bubble baths. Try some fun, new wines.

♥ Build a backyard campfire and roast hot dogs and s'mores for dinner one night.

♥ Visit a local tearoom and go out for an elegant afternoon tea.

"There is no need to go to India or anywhere else to find peace. You will find that deep place of silence right in your own room, your garden, or... your bathtub." ~ROSS

65

"Let's Go Girls" Home Spa Party

Transform your home into a girlfriend's spa getaway for the weekend. Treat your friends to a buffet of indulgences! :)

° Purchase yummy spa products by Crabtree & Evelyn, Caswell Massey OR make your own. ° Clear out your living room, rent or purchase pilates or yoga videos, and take a fitness class. ° SPA GIFT BASKETS: mesh sponges, pumice stones, fun nail polish colors, lipsticks, magazines, & flavored seltzer waters. ° Light candles everywhere. ° Give eachother pedicures, manicures, facials and massages. ° Do a poetry reading. ° Watch "chick flicks" and eat popcorn sprinkled with a little parmesan cheese. ° Set up your CD player and play spa music: anything by Enya, "Romanza", by Andrea Bocelli, and "White Stones," by Secret Garden. ° Make sure everyone brings jammies, slippers, and comfy robes. ° Serve yummy spa cuisine. °

"Most of us dream of being the perfect hostess. This means being well organized far enough ahead of time to allow for a hot bath, a short rest, and time to put on a pretty frock and spray yourself with White Lilac. This never, never happens to me." —Gladys Jaber "Stillmeadow Cookbook" 1947 ♥

In Your Own Words
J O U R N A L

"A #2 pencil and a dream can take you anywhere."

– Joyce Meyers

In Your Own Words
J O U R N A L

"Dost thou love life? Then do not squander time; for that's the stuff life is made of." BENJAMIN FRANKLIN ♥

Your Home Spa Retreat : Body Treatments

"Water is the most healing of all remedies
and the best of all cosmetics."

~Arab Proverb

SMELLS FRESH & WONDERFUL, SUPER HEALING SCALP REMEDY...

Tea Tree Shampoo ♥
& BLEMISH REMOVER POTION

Add 4 drops tea tree oil & 2 drops biotin oil to 3 tablespoons mild, un-scented shampoo. (Try baby shampoo from the health food store.) Combine ingredients. Apply to hair. Leave on for 5 minutes. Rinse. Condition.

here's a little beauty secret...

BLEMISH POTION: Tea tree (also called melaleuca) is also good for keep-ing acne at bay. In a one oz. bottle combine one oz. jojoba oil, 5 drops tea tree oil, 3 drops lavender oil, 5 drops rosemary oil, & 2 drops orange oil. Shake well. Apply a few drops to a cotton ball & dab on blemishes.

"Sabrina fair, listen where thou art sitting under the glassy, cool, translucent wave, in twisted braids of lilies knitting the loose train of thy amber-dropping hair..."
~ JOHN MILTON ♥

Copa Banana-Mango Conditioner

A treat for summer hair that replenishes vitamins and moisture in sun or chlorine-damaged hair.

1.) Combine:
   ½ mashed banana
   ¼ mashed mango
   ¼ mashed papaya
   1 tablespoon honey

2.) Apply to clean, wet hair. Wrap hair up in a towel. Allow conditioner to penetrate hair for half an hour. Rinse well.

"...his flashing eyes, his floating hair, weave a circle round him thrice, and close your eyes with holy dread, for he on honeydew hath fed, and drunk the milk of paradise." - Coleridge

The bee as alchemist...

Queen Bee
honey hair pak

NATURALLY MOISTURIZING AMBROSIA FOR YOUR HAIR.

Combine:
½ cup honey
2 tablespoons olive oil
a dash of cinnamon

Apply to hair. Leave on for ½ hour. Rinse.

"The very honey of all earthly joy."
— COWLEY

POSY HOLDER

A DEEP, PENETRATING CLEANSER AND A PROTECTIVE CONDITIONER ALL IN ONE LITTLE CLAY PAK!

SPA CLAY PAK
FOR HEALTHY TRESSES

White clay is best for hair, while red & green clays are commonly used for body treatments. Coconut oil will soften and protect your hair.

You'll need:
- ½ cup olive oil
- 3 tablespoons coconut oil
- 4 tablespoons powdered white clay
- 1 cup purified water
- 3 drops mango essential oil

Heat oils over low flame until slightly warm to the touch. Remove from heat. In a separate bowl, slowly combine water & clay until it forms a paste. Combine oil mixture & clay mixture. Mix well. Apply to clean, towel-dried hair. Work the mixture over scalp, through hair, and all the way to the ends. Wrap your hair in a towel and allow clay pak to sit in hair for twenty minutes. Wash & condition as you normally would.

Tip: For thicker, healthier hair add biotin and silica to your vitamin regimen. Be sure to run this by your doctor first.

"...weave the sunlight in your hair." T.S. Eliot ♥

North Woods
Warm Maple Sugar
Hair Treatment

BE TRANSPORTED TO A CRISP AUTUMN DAY ... MMMMM....

In a microwave-safe bowl
Combine:
- 2 Tablespoons pure maple Syrup
- 2 Tablespoons molasses

Heat until slightly warm. Wet your hair, and work mixture into it. Allow to sit for ten minutes. Wash and condition as you normally would.

- T.S. ELIOT
"What water lapping the bow, and scent of pine and woodthrush singing through the fog."

This will make you feel like a new woman! ☺

Aromatherapy Neck Roll
& deep breathing exercise for renewal

First: Roll a few sprigs of lavender and five bay leaves in a washcloth. Roll up cloth. Place rolled washcloth in the center of a flattened guest towel so washcloth is laying lengthwise. Roll washcloth up in towel lengthwise and tie off ends with lengths of string or ribbon (like a piece of candy.)

Second: Get into a warm tub with rose petals floating on the surface. Place the neck roll behind your head and let the steam activate the balmy scent of lavender and bay leaves.

Third:
Close your eyes and imagine walking down a garden path with waterfalls, lying on a beach with palm trees waving in the breeze, or sitting in the middle of a golden meadow with the sun warming your face. Now, breathe in through your nose deeply and slowly and feel your diaphragm expand and fill with air. Hold the breath in for a moment before slowly exhaling. Do this several times and feel the tension release.

"A solitary fantasy can totally transform one million realities." ~Maya Angelou

Youthful Yogurt Facial

The mild acid in yogurt balances the pH in your skin as it cleans your face. ♥

Apply ¼ cup plain yogurt to your face. Leave on for twenty minutes. Rinse with warm water and then splash your face with cold water to close pores. Follow up with a rich moisturizing cream. (I love the old fashioned Ponds cold cream).

Lemon Cucumber Spa Water

When my husband Jeff and I were in Maui we visited the gorgeous Grand Wailea Spa. While we were there we were given this glorious spa water to sip. Now you can enjoy this beverage guilt-free in the comfort of your very own at-home spa. ♥

Simply fill a half gallon glass jug with purified water. Add two slices cucumber and two slices lemon to the water. Cover and let chill in the refrigerator for twelve hours before serving.

"She got her looks from her father - he's a plastic surgeon." ☺
GROUCHO MARX ♥

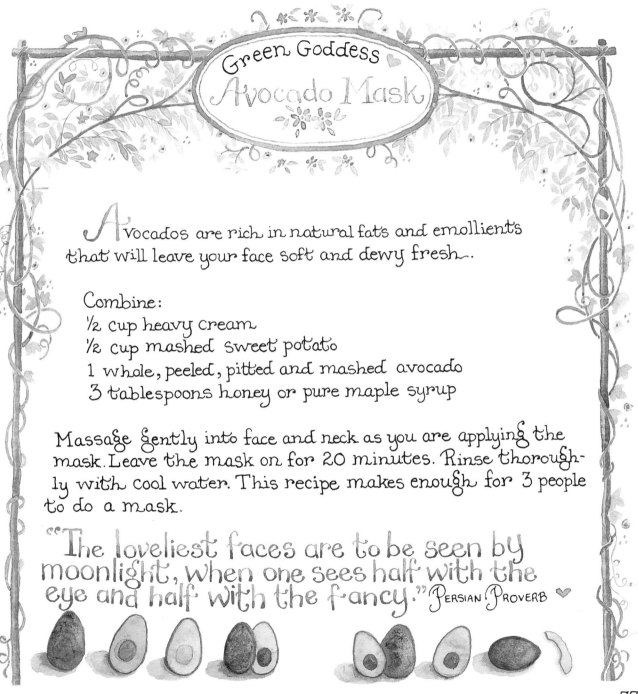

Green Goddess Avocado Mask

Avocados are rich in natural fats and emollients that will leave your face soft and dewy fresh.

Combine:
½ cup heavy cream
½ cup mashed sweet potato
1 whole, peeled, pitted and mashed avocado
3 tablespoons honey or pure maple syrup

Massage gently into face and neck as you are applying the mask. Leave the mask on for 20 minutes. Rinse thoroughly with cool water. This recipe makes enough for 3 people to do a mask.

"The loveliest faces are to be seen by moonlight, when one sees half with the eye and half with the fancy." Persian Proverb ♥

Hawaiian Pina Colada Mask

aloha!

Bromelian is a naturally occuring enzyme found in fresh pineapple. This enzyme gently exfoliates dead skin cells, and the acids in pineapple balance the pH in your skin. Coconut naturally moisturizes.

Combine:
¼ cup crushed, fresh pineapple
2 tablespoons coconut milk

Rub mixture onto face. Leave on for five minutes. Rinse with warm water. Pat dry with a soft towel. Follow up with your favorite moisturizer.

"I'm tired of all this nonsense about beauty only being skin deep. That's deep enough. What do you want, an adorable pancreas?" Jean Kerr ♥

"I believe that the finest vacation would be, to sail away on an ocean of tea..." MP

Green tea beach spritz

This is a terrific little potion to carry with you in your beach bag. Green tea is a small miracle, and is good for you inside and out. Peppermint tea makes this spritz refreshing & cool.

In a plastic spritzer bottle, combine the following ingredients:

1/4 c. strong green tea
1/4 c. strong peppermint tea

Set the spritzer bottle on the "mist" setting & use all over to freshen up.

Cocoa Java Body Polish

"BEHIND EVERY SUCCESSFUL WOMAN - IS A SUBSTANTIAL AMOUNT OF COFFEE." -PIRO

This is one of my favorite body treatments! The rich scents of creamy cocoa & chocolate are pure decadence. Try this treatment in the shower instead of the tub because it's a little messy. Trust me, it's worth it! It will make your skin SO soft!

In a small, glass bowl combine :
¼ cup freshly ground coffee beans
    3 tablespoons white sugar
        2 teaspoons unsweetened, powdered cocoa
        2 tablespoons olive oil
        1 tablespoon water

Mix well. Step into shower & wet your entire body. Massage body polish all over, avoiding face and genital area. Rinse well with warm water. ♥

Brown Sugar Coconut Body Glow

Fresh coconut gently exfoliates, and brown sugar gives you a bit of a deeper exfoliating treatment without being too harsh and abrasive.

Combine:

1 cup dark brown sugar
½ cup freshly grated coconut
¼ cup coconut oil, melted
1 tablespoon honey
1 teaspoon vitamin E oil
10 drops coconut perfume oil
3 drops sandalwood essential oil
3 drops vanilla essential oil

Standing on a towel, rub mixture all over your body. Allow the body-glow to penetrate skin for three to five minutes. Rub mixture off with a damp hand towel. Soak in the tub or take a shower to rinse off remaining mixture.

"Love yourself first and everything else falls into line. You really have to love yourself to get anything done in this world."
— Lucille Ball

Arabian Night's Chai Bath Soak

In order to fully experience this sweet, intoxicating bath, you have to set the scene in your bathroom. Light lots of earthy scented candles (like sandalwood, patchouli, & eucalyptus), treat yourself to a big, red bath towel, and listen to gentle guitar music. Hang a buttery-soft silk robe on the back of your bathroom door so you can continue to feel luxurious and pampered even after you get out of the tub.

In a small, glass bowl combine:
· 1 cup olive oil*
· ½ cup honey
· ¼ cup vanilla shower gel
· 10 drops sandalwood essential oil
*(for a more "bubbly" bath, omit olive oil.)

In a small muslin bag combine:
· 1 teaspoon ground cloves
· 1 tablespoon ground nutmeg
· 1 tablespoon ground cardamom
· 1 tablespoon ground cinnamon

While you are filling the tub, pour the oil mixture under the running water. Next, tie the spice bag around the faucet, directly under the running water. Soak as long as you like.

a magic carpet ride...

"A bubble bath with a magazine behind a locked door at the end of a hectic day is the equivalent of a day at Elizabeth Arden without the wasted time, money and guilt." ALEXANDRA STODDARD ♥

Luscious Body Butter
Super moisturizing. Great for after tanning.

You'll Need :
2 tablespoons grated beeswax
2 teaspoons purified water
½ cup grated cocoa butter
4 tablespoons sesame oil
1 tablespoon coconut oil
1 tablespoon olive oil
10 drops mango perfume oil
(or your favorite scent) ☺

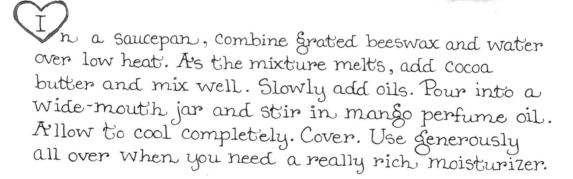

In a saucepan, combine grated beeswax and water over low heat. As the mixture melts, add cocoa butter and mix well. Slowly add oils. Pour into a wide-mouth jar and stir in mango perfume oil. Allow to cool completely. Cover. Use generously all over when you need a really rich moisturizer.

" [I wish I could] have back up singers echo me every time I say something important." BARBARA ANN KIPFER
The Wish List

83

Tangerine Dream Hand Cream

Smells fruity & heavenly. Feels delicious on dry, chapped hands. Great on elbows & knees, too!

In a small container, combine:
4 tablespoons thick hand cream (like Nivea)
2 tablespoons cocoa butter cream
4 drops tangerine essential or perfume oil

Mix well. Cover.

"I carry the sun in a golden cup, the moon in a silver bag." WILLIAM BUTLER YEATS

Fizzing Soda Pop Bath Bomb

THESE WILL MAKE CUTE PARTY FAVORS AT YOUR NEXT HOME-SPA PARTY! ♥

Bath bombs are so fun to use and they smell great ~ An instant effervescent bath as soon as they hit the water. This bath bomb recipe was inspired by 7-UP lemon-lime soda pop.

You'll need:
- 1 cup baking soda
- ½ cup citric acid
- ½ cup cornstarch
- 2 teaspoons shea butter, melted
- 1 tablespoon sweet almond oil
- ½ teaspoon lemon fragrance oil
- ½ teaspoon lime fragrance oil
- 1 spritzer bottle full of witch hazel liquid

Mix baking soda, citric acid & cornstarch together in a big glass bowl. Add melted shea butter, almond oil & fragrance oil. Spray mixture with witch hazel until it gets clumpy and sticks together. Form mixture into balls with your hands. Allow to dry overnight. Wrap in waxed paper or Ziploc bags until ready to use.

"O the moon shone bright on Mrs. Porter and her daughter...they wash their feet in soda water." - T.S. Eliot ♥

85

Bonita Margarita
hand treatment

Have you ever seen the movie *Like Water for Chocolate*? If not, this is the perfect time to sit back and watch this sexy, artsy movie and treat yourself to a revitalizing hand treatment... and then maybe take a siesta. ☺

In a small, glass ramekin, combine:
4 mashed strawberries
3 tablespoons white sugar
1 tablespoon tequila
A little lime zest

Wet hands with warm water. Slowly massage the strawberry mixture all over your hands. Rinse thoroughly with warm water.

"Sweet Genevieve, the days may come, the days may go, but still the hands of memory weave the blissful dreams of long ago." - GEORGE COOPER

Hydrotherapy for Hands, Feet & Body ♥

Hydrotherapy, or "water healing" is an ancient method for curing a variety of ailments. Water has the power to make us feel better. Just sitting in a hot tub at the end of the day is proof that water can work wonders for your body and mind. The Romans created glorious communal baths with pillars of marble and rose petals strewn everywhere for a soothing effect.

Here is a mini-hydrotherapy treatment for your hands & feet. Feel free to try a whole-body hydrotherapy treatment sometime. It is one of the most inexpensive, effective treatments for making one feel better.

Fill one basin with water as hot as your hands or feet can take, and another basin with ice water. Plunge hands or feet in the hot water for 50 to 60 seconds, and then plunge into ice water for 20 seconds. Do this for 10 minutes, alternating

hot and cold, ending with the cold. The heat is relaxing, the cold is stimulating, and both help circulation. The combination is great for treating arthritis or hands that are cramped from typing or gardening. This is an especially good foot treatment for someone who stands on their feet all day.

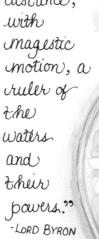

"She looks like a sea Cybele, fresh from ocean, rising with her tiara of proud towers at airy distance, with magestic motion, a ruler of the waters and their powers."
-Lord Byron

♥

87

Spa Hand Therapy
WITH WARMING MITTS ♥

This is a great treatment if you really feel like you have to get away from everything, and you only have a half hour to do it.

You'll need:
3 vitamin E capsules
1 tablespoon aloe vera gel
2 tablespoons plain yogurt
1 tablespoon apricot kernel oil
2 plastic baggies
2 terrycloth spa mitts or 2 new oven mitts

Light candles, and put on some relaxing music. Break open the vitamin E capsules and squeeze them out into a small bowl. Add the aloe, yogurt, and apricot kernel oil to the bowl. Mix well. Rub the mixture all over your hands. Put a plastic baggie on each hand, and then the spa mitts. Sit back in a comfortable chair for a half hour and close your eyes. When the half hour is up, remove baggies & mitts from your hands. Rinse hands thoroughly. Follow up with your Tangerine Dream Hand Cream.

"A multitude of small delights constitute happiness." ♥
- Charles Baudelaire

Rosemary Foot Bath ♥

Revitalizing rosemary & naturally deodorizing tea tree... happy feet.

Pour cold water in a large basin, filling it about 2/3 from the top. Add 2 sprigs fresh rosemary, 10 drops tea tree oil, 10 drops rosemary oil, 10 ice cubes, and a sprinkle of epsom salt. Stir to evenly distribute the oil in the basin. Soak feet for 10 minutes. Massage feet while they are still in the basin, using firm, deliberate strokes. Dry them off vigorously with a rough towel for one minute. Doing this will improve circulation in your feet. ♥

"What flowers are at my feet...what soft incense hangs upon the Bough." ~ John Keats

89

♥ Strawberries & Champagne Foot Spa

WIGGLE YOUR TOES IN THIS SLIPPERY FOOT BATH. MMMMM... ☺

In a basin, combine:
3 (3-oz) boxes strawberry Jell-O
3 cups Champagne

Stir with a wire whisk until mixed.
Dip your feet in & wiggle your toes ☺
Rinse feet well. Pat dry.   ♥

Marble Foot Massage

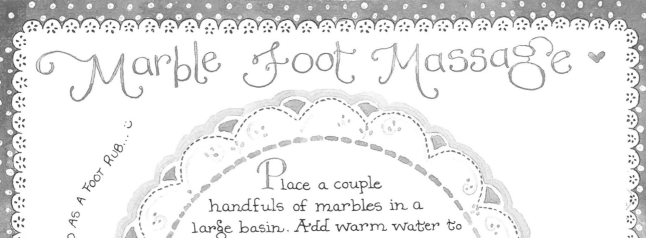

ALMOST AS GOOD AS A FOOT RUB... ;)

Place a couple handfuls of marbles in a large basin. Add warm water to cover your feet. Add fresh herbs & flowers to the basin if you wish. Run feet on top of marbles for a gentle foot massage. Do this for at least ten minutes. Pat feet dry with a towel. Rub peppermint foot lotion on your feet to complete the treatment.

♥

"Every object, every being is a jar full of delight. Be a connoisseur."
— Rumi

Romantic Edible Massage Oil

For a romantic rendezvous or a special Valentine's Day treat, mix up some of this massage oil for the love of your life. This recipe has all-natural ingredients and is fun to experiment with. ♥

In a clean glass bottle combine:
4 oz. apricot kernel oil
4 oz. almond oil
a few drops vitamin E oil
1 teaspoon pure flavor extract (such as vanilla, coconut, or cherry.)
10 oz. pure vegetable, liquid glycerine

Cover and shake gently to mix. Glycerine will separate, so you'll need to shake it before each use.

<u>Fun idea</u>: Think of a secluded spot in your yard such as a gazebo or a screened-in porch to set up a massage table. Give your love a massage in the fresh air. While it's raining, it can be very romantic too. ♥

"If all the world and love were young, And truth in every shepherd's tongue, these pretty pleasures might me move to live with thee, and be thy love." ~ Sir Walter Raleigh ♥

& Honey Dust ♥

Sprinkle this seductive honey dust anywhere you want to kiss or be kissed. Honey and vanilla powder can both be purchased at either your local health food store or online.

In an air-tight tin, combine:
1 cup cornstarch
2 tablespoons vanilla powder
3 tablespoons honey powder

Tip: I found honey and vanilla powder at www.fragrancesupplies.com and all kinds of hard to find spa recipe ingredients, containers & fun, easy spa recipes at www.lavenderlane.com. Oh! I can't forget to mention my friends at Watkins! They carry some of the best prod~ucts I've ever used! Go to www.watkinsonline.com. ☺

"All thoughts, all passions, all delights,
Whatever stirs this mortal frame,
All are but ministers of love,
And feed his sacred flame."
- SAMUEL TAYLOR COLERIDGE ♥

93

Beach Babe Suntan Oil ♥

This is an extremely rich and exotic tanning oil with a touch of Hawaiian romance. I use it when I go to the beach, and as a daily all-over moisturizer in the summer.

Combine:

8 oz. almond oil
15 drops coconut perfume oil
6 drops plumeria perfume oil
4 drops mango perfume oil
3 drops passion fruit or guava perfume oil

Caution: This tanning oil contains no sunscreen and will not prevent sunburn. Don't use this on babies or small children. ♥

Mix well, and using a funnel, decant into a dark brown glass bottle with a tight fitting lid.

"I worry that the person who thought up Muzak may be thinking up something else." —Lily Tomlin ♥

94

MAUI LIP GLOSS

For yummy, kissable lips:
2 teaspoons grated cocoa butter
2 teaspoons coconut oil
4 teaspoons macadamia nut oil
1/8 teaspoon almond oil
A few drops of the flavored oil of your choice (the kind you can buy wherever candy-making supplies are sold)

Combine all ingredients in micro-wave safe bowl. Heat just until melted. Mix well. Pour into a small container. Cool.

"I WENT TO MAUI TO STAY A WEEK AND REMAINED FIVE. I NEVER SPENT SO PLEASANT A MONTH BEFORE, OR BADE ANY PLACE GOODBYE SO REGRETFULLY. I HAVE NOT ONCE THOUGHT OF BUSINESS, OR CARE OR HUMAN TOIL OR TROUBLE OR SORROW OR WEARINESS AND THE MEMORY OF IT WILL REMAIN WITH ME ALWAYS." Mark Twain

There is an interesting phenomenon called the "Proust Effect" that I came across while taking a psychology class. This is simply memories and emotions being prompted by a scent. Example: Picture yourself walking down a city street and as you pass a bakery the scent of chocolate chip cookies overwhelms you. You immediately feel as though you've been transported back in time to your mother's kitchen. The scent brings tears to your eyes because you miss your mom. This is the Proust Effect.

Ever since this psych lesson, I've been using this little trick in my own life to create a sort of "Scrapbook of Scents." I do this whenever I travel or plan on experiencing something new. This is one of my favorite things to do. It really keeps the memory of certain experiences, places and people alive.

The next time you're planning a vacation, select a new perfume scent that is unlike anything you've ever worn before. DO NOT wear this new scent until you arrive at your vacation spot. While on vacation, wear this perfume every day. When you get home, don't wear the perfume for 2 weeks. The next time you smell it you will be back at the place you were vacationing. The scent will remind you of this place forever! ☺

Anytime I want to escape, my perfumes serve as a sort of time machine. When I wear "Summer Hill" by Crabtree & Evelyn, I'm on Nantucket Island. When I wear "Rapture" by Victoria's Secret, it's my wedding day again. And when I wear "Savannah Gardens" by Crabtree & Evelyn, I'm sitting on the rocks high over the North Shore of Lake Superior, having coffee with my mom and watching the sunrise ☺ ♥ Hi Mom!

"Put the Lime in the Coconut" Perfume Mist

"The ideal of beauty is simplicity and tranquility." - von Goethe

This is a fun scent for summer, a vacation by the beach, or when going out to a festive restaurant or party.

Fill an 8 oz spritzer bottle 3/4 from the top with Everclear. Add 2 tablespoons purified water, 15 drops lime perfume oil, & 15 drops coconut perfume oil. Cover. Shake gently.

This recipe can be used with any of your favorite scents, not just lime and coconut. Making your own perfume mist is fun! Don't be afraid to experiment.

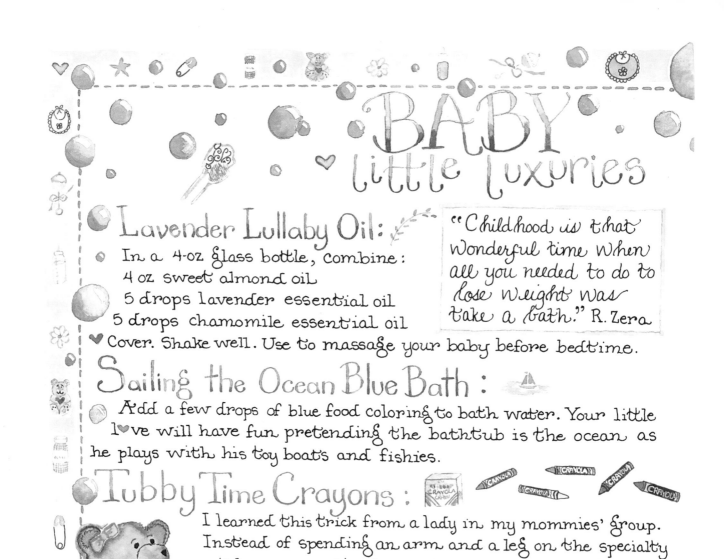

BABY
little luxuries

Lavender Lullaby Oil:

In a 4-oz glass bottle, combine:
4 oz sweet almond oil
5 drops lavender essential oil
5 drops chamomile essential oil

Cover. Shake well. Use to massage your baby before bedtime.

> "Childhood is that wonderful time when all you needed to do to lose weight was take a bath." R. Zera

Sailing the Ocean Blue Bath:

Add a few drops of blue food coloring to bath water. Your little love will have fun pretending the bathtub is the ocean as he plays with his toy boats and fishies.

Tubby Time Crayons:

I learned this trick from a lady in my mommies' group. Instead of spending an arm and a leg on the specialty tub crayons, simply purchase a box of the big, chunky, <u>washable</u> Crayola crayons. They work just as well and wash off the side of the tub in a flash.

BUBBLES
for your little love

Awesome Bubble Potion:

This recipe makes the very best bubbles! The tub is a great place to let your kids blow bubbles.

- ⅓ cup dishwashing liquid (such as Dawn)
- ½ gallon water
- 2 tablespoons glycerine
- A sprinkle of sugar

♥ Mix all ingredients in a big bowl. Pour solution into a big, clean, plastic jug. Transfer to small, plastic bubble bottles as needed.

After-Bath Fairy Dust : (for kids age 4 and up)

- ¼ cup cornstarch
- 2 teaspoons baby powder
- ⅛ teaspoon fine, multi-colored glitter

♥ Mix ingredients in a small container with a cover. Sprinkle anywhere you want to add some sparkle, except for your face.

"Babies don't need a vacation but I still see them at the beach. I'll go up to them and say, "What are you doing here? You've never worked a day in your life!" " — STEVEN WRIGHT ♥ ☺

Home Sweet Home Mist
FOR SWEETLY SCENTED ROOMS

The crisp scents of apple & orange mingle with the warm scents of cinnamon & vanilla - it's like autumn in a bottle.

Fill an 8 oz spritzer bottle almost to the top with purified water. Top off with 3 tablespoons vodka & the following oils :

10 drops apple scented oil
7 drops orange scented oil
5 drops cinnamon essential oil
3 drops vanilla essential oil

Cover bottle with the spray top. Shake gently. Spray generously around all the rooms of your home sweet home.

"There is something in the autumn that is native to my blood - Touch of manner, hint of mood, and my is like a rhyme, With the yellow & the purple & crimson keeping time."
- BLISS CARMAN

♪♫ Whistle while you work... ♪♫

Lemon & Mint
W I N D O W · W A S H

Enjoy the refreshing scents of
lemon & mint as you make your
windows squeaky clean! ♥

In a glass spray bottle, combine:
Juice from one lemon
2 cups club soda
½ teaspoon peppermint essential oil
1 teaspoon cornstarch

Use in place of commercial
window cleaner. Shake gently
before each use. ♥

"By happy alchemy
of mind they turn to
pleasure all they find."
– Matthew Green ♥

Sweet & Savory Spa Cuisine

"The implements of the little feast had been disposed upon the lawn of an old English country house, in what I should call the perfect middle of a splendid afternoon."
- Henry James *Portrait of a Lady*

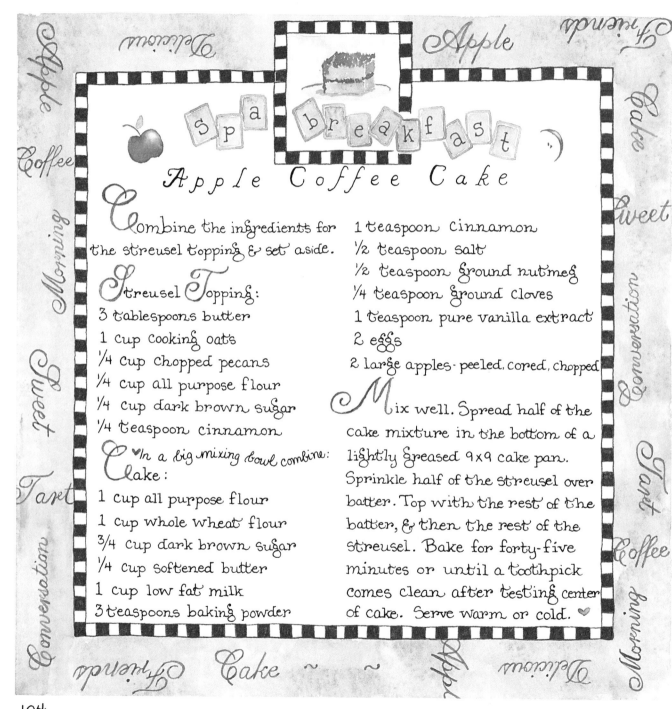

Spa breakfast

Apple Coffee Cake

Combine the ingredients for the streusel topping & set aside.

Streusel Topping:
3 tablespoons butter
1 cup cooking oats
1/4 cup chopped pecans
1/4 cup all purpose flour
1/4 cup dark brown sugar
1/4 teaspoon cinnamon

♥ In a big mixing bowl combine:
Cake:
1 cup all purpose flour
1 cup whole wheat flour
3/4 cup dark brown sugar
1/4 cup softened butter
1 cup low fat milk
3 teaspoons baking powder
1 teaspoon cinnamon
1/2 teaspoon salt
1/2 teaspoon ground nutmeg
1/4 teaspoon ground cloves
1 teaspoon pure vanilla extract
2 eggs
2 large apples - peeled, cored, chopped

Mix well. Spread half of the cake mixture in the bottom of a lightly greased 9x9 cake pan. Sprinkle half of the streusel over batter. Top with the rest of the batter, & then the rest of the streusel. Bake for forty-five minutes or until a toothpick comes clean after testing center of cake. Serve warm or cold. ♥

104

Festive Fruit Gazpacho

A DELIGHTFUL FIRST COURSE FOR A GARDEN PARTY, OR A LIGHT DESSERT. MAKES 6 SERVINGS.

You'll need:

- ♥ ½ cup fresh strawberries, chopped
- ♥ ½ cup fresh raspberries or blackberries
- ♥ ½ cup fresh pineapple, chopped
- ♥ 1 cup grapes, quartered
- ♥ ¾ cup fresh blueberries
- ♥ 1 cup white grape juice
- ♥ ½ cup freshly squeezed orange juice
- ♥ ¼ teaspoon freshly ground black pepper

Combine all ingredients and fold together gently. Spoon into six martini glasses. Garnish with mint sprigs, orange peel spirals, & pansies.

"No diet will remove all the fat from your body because the brain is entirely fat. Without a brain you might _look_ good, but all you could _do_ is run for public office."

— George Bernard Shaw ♥

Thai Chicken Pita Pizza

This is the BEST pizza I've ever eaten. It's not exactly low fat, but there are lots of good-for-you ingredients in this little pizza. ♥

Ingredients for Chicken: ♥
- 12 oz boneless, skinless chicken breast cut into small, bite-size cubes
- 2 tablespoons extra virgin olive oil

Pizza toppings & crust: ♥
- For the crust, use small, round pitas that have been rubbed with a little olive oil & cornmeal on the bottom.
- 2 cups mozzarella cheese, shredded
- 6 scallions, chopped
- ½ cup mung bean sprouts
- ¼ cup carrots, julienned
- Peanuts
- 2 tablespoons fresh cilantro, chopped
- bottled peanut sauce

Assembling pizzas: ♥
In a skillet, cook the chicken in the olive oil until cooked through. Chill in the refrigerator.

Lay six prepared pitas on a pizza stone. Spread a couple tablespoons peanut sauce on each pita. Divide the cheese, chicken, scallions, sprouts, & carrots on the pitas. Top each with a little more mozzarella & a sprinkle of peanuts. Bake in 425-degree oven until golden and the cheese is bubbly. (about ten minutes). Remove pizzas from oven. Sprinkle each with a little of the fresh cilantro. Serve each pizza with a small ramekin of hot peanut sauce for pouring over the pizza.

"Nothing takes the ♥ taste out of peanut butter quite like unrequited love." ♥

♥

♥ Charles M. Schulz - Charlie Brown

Leaning Tower of Pisa
Spinach Lasagna

Sophia Loren said, "Everything you see I owe to spaghetti." And while this may be true, I believe lasagna is a beautifier as well— as long as you don't eat the whole pan ! ☺

Ingredients:
10 oz package frozen spinach, chopped
15 oz container lowfat ricotta cheese
2 cloves fresh garlic, minced
4 carrots, sliced ¼ inch thick
3 cups broccoli, cut into small pieces
8 oz package no-boil lasagna noodles
26 oz jar marinara sauce
12 oz grated mozzarella cheese
½ cup freshly grated parmesan cheese

Thaw spinach & drain WELL. Mix with ricotta & garlic. Steam veggies 'til tender. Drain. Place ⅓ of the sauce in bottom of 13"x 9" pan, then a layer of noodles, ½ the ricotta mixture, veggies, parmesan, & ⅓ mozzarella. Repeat with rest of ing., ending with sauce & mozzarella. Bake at 350° for 35 minutes. Cool 15 minutes.

107

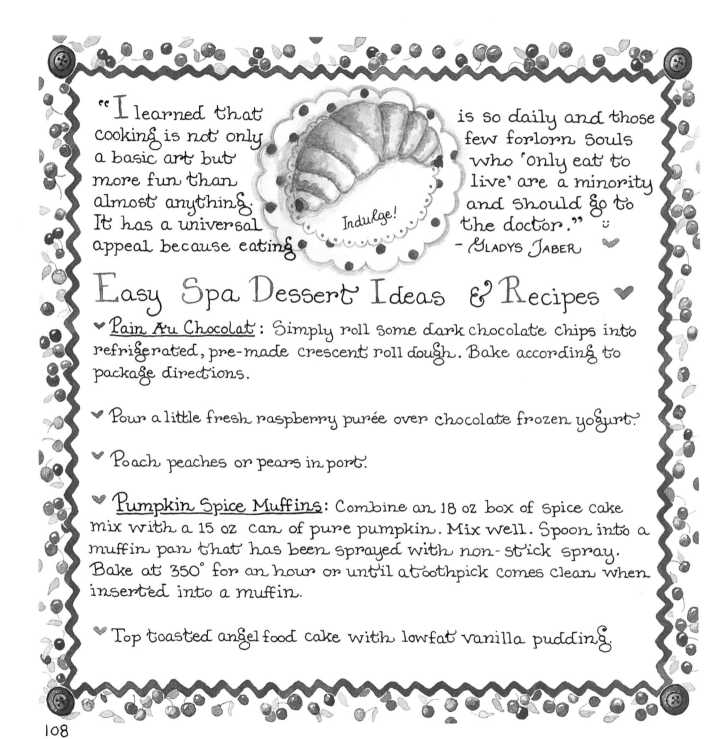

"I learned that cooking is not only a basic art but more fun than almost anything. It has a universal appeal because eating is so daily and those few forlorn souls who 'only eat to live' are a minority and should go to the doctor." ☺
— Gladys Jaber 🖤

Easy Spa Dessert Ideas & Recipes 🖤

🖤 <u>Pain Au Chocolat</u>: Simply roll some dark chocolate chips into refrigerated, pre-made crescent roll dough. Bake according to package directions.

🖤 Pour a little fresh raspberry purée over chocolate frozen yogurt.

🖤 Poach peaches or pears in port.

🖤 <u>Pumpkin Spice Muffins</u>: Combine an 18 oz box of spice cake mix with a 15 oz can of pure pumpkin. Mix well. Spoon into a muffin pan that has been sprayed with non-stick spray. Bake at 350° for an hour or until a toothpick comes clean when inserted into a muffin.

🖤 Top toasted angel food cake with lowfat vanilla pudding.

Also by Melissa Placzek

CHIN DEEP IN BUBBLES
By Melissa Placzek
ISBN: 1-931412-44-8
$12.95 (£7.99)
Paperback; 112 pages
Available wherever books are sold

"This book is a celebration of pampering. It's full of just the kind of indulgences every woman deserves…You're going to relish every one of these simple luxuries."
—Country Homes and Gardens Book Club

"…a book designed for that handy-in-the-kitchen, make-it-simple, make-it-special crowd. It's a book about relaxing. It's a book about self-indulgence."
—The Forest Lake Press

Every woman deserves to be pampered, and *Chin Deep in Bubbles* is written in that spirit. The heady scents, lavish textures, and warm rewards of the easy home-spa recipes in this book will make your world a prettier, more comfortable place. This unique book will inspire you to indulge in life's little luxuries with wonderful baths, facials, hair treatments, aromatherapy, delicious spa cuisine and more.

Throughout the book you'll find useful health tips, fun ideas, and simple pleasures that will be sure to enrich your personal time.

All these recipes are easy and will fill your home with the wafting scents of Mother Nature's most wonderful aromas, including coffee, lemon, chocolate, and jasmine. Perfect for a cold snowy day as well as the evening after a long day's work, *Chin Deep in Bubbles* is a trip to paradise, one you can take over and over again.